ANNETTE ROEDER

# Olaf Hajek
# VEGGIE POWER

PRESTEL

Munich • London • New York

# Veggie Power

## or 'What is a vegetable?'

Bruno doesn't like capsicum, Lisa doesn't care for asparagus. And Anton doesn't like any vegetables at all. 'I don't eat anything that's green', he says and pushes some red beets to the side of his plate. Why should any of us eat vegetables? Is it just because our parents say so? Well, vegetables may not look all that exciting, but there's a lot more to carrots, pumpkins and potatoes than meets the eye!

What are vegetables, really? The word comes from an older term, *vegetabilis*, which means 'capable of life and growth'. In former times, cooks considered anything that originated from plants and needed to be cooked and seasoned to be 'vegetables'. Other plant foods, such as apples or pears, had enough flavor of their own due to a high sugar content. They were given a different name: 'fruits'. This way of dividing the two food types, however, is a bit old-fashioned because tastes have changed over time. People no longer cook everything to a pulp, and some even eat peeled kohlrabi as they would an apple. Some fruits, moreover, are rarely eaten raw. You'd probably try raw quince only once before spitting it out! However, this doesn't mean that kohlrabi should become a fruit and quince a vegetable.

Scientists prefer to be a little more precise about naming plant groups. Botanists are scientists who specialize in plants, and they set completely different guidelines for distinguishing a fruit from a vegetable. Scientifically, the 'fruit' of a plant is the part that forms from the blossom of its flower and contains one or more seeds. Think of a peach, a pear and some red currants. All of them have seeds hidden within. In fact, it's very rare for seeds to stick out of a fruit, as you'd find with a strawberry. Botanical fruits, moreover, are often sold with part of the plant's stalk (or stem base) still attached – which shows how the fruit has grown out of its stem.

Now that you know what a botanical fruit is, how might you figure out whether someone had put a fruit or a vegetable on your plate? The easiest way is to discover what part of the plant it is. Are you looking at a thick root, a gnarled tuber, a pale shoot, a flat leaf or an elongated stem?

If it's any of these plant parts, then you've definitely been given a vegetable. Such foods include beets, potatoes, asparagus, spinach or even rhubarb. That's correct! You haven't misread anything – rhubarb is also a vegetable. Chefs, of course, have always known this to be true, and they cook rhubarb with lots of sugar in the pot.

But what if you've been served the part of a plant that botanists call a fruit? Is this a food you'd always recognize as a fruit? That's when things get a little more complicated. In cooking, we regard botanical fruits that come from 'annuals' (or plants that die off every year after ripening) as vegetables. These foods include zucchini, peppers and pumpkins. They also include melons, which taste so sweet and are popular in fruit salads. In order to harvest them, such vegetables need to be sown anew in spring each year. On the other hand, when a botanical fruit grows from a 'perennial' – a plant that is several or even many, many years old, with flowers that produce new fruit year after year – then it is certainly a food fruit as well. Orange trees, apple trees and raspberry bushes are all perennials, and they often become woody with age.

There's one botanical fruit, however, that has a special place in the world of fruits and vegetables. Little princess tomato is mainly cultivated as an 'annual' in Europe, but it actually grows on plant branches for years on end in its warm homelands of South and Central America. Therefore, many Europeans consider it a vegetable and many Latin Americans consider it a fruit. Other people see the tomato as a kind of double-agent – taking its place in both the fruit and vegetable communities! It's probably best, however, to let garden experts quarrel among themselves about the tomato. At least now you can tell the difference, more or less, between fruits and vegetables. And that means you already know more than many people do … even if you sometimes forget the exceptions.

What's most exciting about vegetables and fruits are the many things you can do with them. Veggies can be used for purposes other than soup. They can appear in clothes and concerts, energy and great art! You don't believe it? Then let's begin an exploration. Olaf Hajek, the famous illustrator, has painted his favorite vegetables for you. And in every one of his pictures, he tells you a fairy tale as well. Take your time and appreciate how much fun Olaf's marvelous stories are. And if you want to find out more about each vegetable, you can read the texts accompanying each picture. I've also included some interesting, funny and practically unbelievable facts. Maybe your grandpa's vegetable soup will not taste as bland when you've read all this!

Have lots of fun exploring this book … and here's wishing you 'Bon Appetit'!

**Annette Roeder**

# Carrots and Parsnips

One of them glows like the rising sun, while the other could do with shaving off its yellow stubble. So why does this odd couple, the carrot and the parsnip, share a chapter in our book? Even if it's hard to recognize at first glance, they both have a lot in common. Both come from a plant family known as umbellifers, and both grow from the same parts of their plants: the roots. You can pull these roots out of the ground in summer and fall and make almost anything with them, such as salads, soups, syrups, cakes and even beer. Carrot and parsnip baby foods are especially popular, as they taste pleasantly sweet without any additives and are easy to digest. And if you feel creative, you can carve a flute for yourself out of these versatile roots. Members of the Vienna Vegetable Orchestra know all about this, as they play with instruments made exclusively from vegetables!

Like all odd couples, the carrot and the parsnip have very different histories. The yellow parsnip is much, much older than the orange-colored carrot. Neolithic people were cultivating it thousands of years ago, making it one of humankind's oldest crops. Carrots also go back to ancient times, but the orange carrot is something of a 'young gun' among vegetables. It was developed around 500 years ago by crossing white and red root types to make its striking orange color. According to legend, the first orange carrots were grown to honor a 16th-century Dutch king named William of Orange. The parsnip also had a famous royal fan. Ancient Roman Emperor Tiberius was so crazy for parsnips that he had them carted off from the fierce European regions of Germania. Later on, as the potato became popular in the 18th century, parsnips went out of fashion in many parts of Europe. No one wanted to eat them anymore. It wasn't until the 1990's, when organic farmers began to grow older vegetable types, that parsnip fame began to take off again. The carrot, however, has never been out of fashion, and it remains the most popular root vegetable. Some growers even compete for who can grow the heaviest or longest carrot. The current heavyweight champion weighs in at more than 20 pounds (9 kilograms), and the longest one measured just under 18 feet (5.5 meters). Will these records ever be broken?

**Edible parts of the plants:**
The roots can be eaten raw and cooked, and even the fine leaves taste aromatic!

**Some tasty varieties of these root vegetables:**
Danvers, Nantes, Chantenay, imperator, ball and baby carrots, countess, gladiator, hollow crown, and white king parsnips

# Aubergine (Eggplant)

Imagine giant-sized berries hanging from shrubby plants – some with shades of midnight blue or eggshell yellow; others with purple and white stripes. Aubergines are like nothing else, even if the most common varieties are only about 8 inches (20.3 cm) long and have a shape similar to that of a pear. By the way, aubergine is pronounced like 'oh-bear-jean'. It's a French word that's become the standard name for the plant in Germany and Britain. In the USA and other English-speaking countries, these smooth fruits are called eggplants, though this term seems appropriate only for the white, spherical variety. Austrians use the name 'melanzana', a word derived from the Italian 'melanzane', which in turn stems from the original Latin: 'mala insana', or 'bad apple'!

Although they have been popular in Asia for over 4,000 years, aubergines were long viewed with suspicion in Europe. Perhaps this is because they belong to the night-shade family of plants, most of which are poisonous. In fact, the leaves and unripe fruit of the aubergine do contain traces of solanine, a poison that can give you an upset stomach.

During the Middle Ages, people thought that eggplants would make you feel sad. This false rumor likely began because the fruits tasted bitter when raw, had a dark skin and turned black when you cut into them. Another false notion about eggplants claimed they were as unhealthy as cigarettes. Like their nightshade cousin, tobacco, eggplants contain nicotine. However, the amount of nicotine in eggplants is so tiny that you would need to eat over 40 pounds (18 kg) of them to get the same nicotine content from one cigarette. And those 40 pounds would have to be raw fruit, because the nicotine disappears when you cook eggplant.

When prepared in a healthy way, the eggplant can be made into delicious meals. Many cultures around the world have their own special eggplant recipes. My favorite is the Turkish dish, 'Imam-bayildi'. This name, which means 'the Imam fainted', refers to a little tale about an Islamic holy man (or Imam) who tried eggplant stuffed with tomatoes and onions. Out of sheer enthusiasm, he passed out and saw paradise!

**Edible parts of the plant:**
Its flesh is edible, but it must be cooked.

**Varieties of eggplant:**
Rosa Bianca, Japanese white egg, lavender touch, black knight, Violetta di Firenze

# Cauliflower

The name says it all – a cauliflower is a flower! Strictly speaking, it's the bud of the flower that has not yet opened. Cauliflower farmers normally harvest their crop after only 60 days of growth, when the immature buds on each cauliflower head are still white and packed closely together. This is the stage in the cauliflower's life when it's harvested and eaten as a vegetable. If for some reason, however, the farmers decide to let their cauliflower plants continue growing, then the buds' individual florets will drift apart and produce lots of yellow blossoms!

Some of the earliest known cauliflowers probably came from Cyprus or Crete, and by the 16th century the vegetable had been brought to other parts of Europe. Soon, both children and grown-ups learned that cauliflower caused a lot less gas than cabbage or other vegetables. They didn't have to fart so much after enjoying a cauliflower meal!

There is a famous cauliflower recipe named after Madame du Barry, one of the many mistresses of King Louis XIV in France. His other mistresses were probably green, or even yellow, with envy; so it's not surprising that this recipe features cooked cauliflower with a yellowish cheese topping. Even if it now seems rather unflattering to have such a colorless dish named after you, the rule in those days was: the paler, the more elegant!

Most cauliflowers are elegantly white. But they only stay that way if kept out of the sun. This is why traditional farmers painstakingly tie the plant's large leaves together over the heads. Recently, however, some cutting-edge gardeners have cultivated plants that naturally wrap their leaves around the bud, thus saving them a huge amount of work. And now that color has come back in fashion, maybe it's time for white cauliflowers to get a makeover! If only growers could allow the cauliflower more light and maybe cross it with, say, red cabbage. Then, our pale bud could glow in the most beautiful shades, from purple to orange to yellow! That said, there is rhythm in a cauliflower's florets. If you'd like to see and hear it for yourself, just take a peek at the 'Bloemkoolsamba' by Dutch youth music theater Samba Salad!

**Edible parts of the plant:**
People mainly eat the bud or head of the plant, together with the stem –
and even the leaves can be used in good dishes.

**Cauliflower varieties:**
Rushmore, white passion, snow crown, Jesi, Cassius

# Beets

Many children – and even a good number of adults – do not like the taste of this purple-reddish underground stem. They say it tastes 'earthy', although most of them probably don't know the true flavor of soil! Traditionally, beets have been prepared in ways that many find boring, such as cooking them till they turn soft and then cutting them into mushy slices to put next to the roast. But beets are extremely healthy for you, and they can be prepared many different ways. When grated raw, for example, they can taste really fresh; and the plant's young leaves, which are just as healthy as the tuber itself, are delicious in salads.

If you don't like salads, you can do things with beets that don't involve food at all. Try coloring your hair blazing red with the juice of a beetroot, just as English ladies did in centuries past. On the other hand, if your parents don't give you permission to do this because they prefer your hair color the way it is, you could always use beet dye to turn Easter eggs pink! Keep in mind, though, that beet stains on your fingers usually last about a day, and it would be better not to wear your new white T-shirt when doing beet experiments. By the way, you can also use beets to make your pee look impressively red, but you would have to eat a whole beetroot to do this.

As a vegetable expert, you should not confuse tubers with root vegetables, even if they are quite similar. Tubers are thickened structures that often develop from the shaft of the plant's shoot – an area between the root and the leaf covering above the bud. Plants can use them as a food reserve for lean and drier times. With beets, the tuber occurs right under the first leaf of the seed plant, which means that most of them grow underground – even though they are not true roots.

In 1975, this vegetable made its way into space when Russian cosmonauts and American astronauts met there for the very first time and cooked for each other. And what do you think the cosmonauts put on the menu in their Soyuz space capsule? It was borscht, of course… a beetroot soup that is also a national dish in Eastern Europe!

**Edible parts of the plant:**
The tuber is delicious both cooked and raw, and the young leaves are used as a salad.

**Tasty varieties of beets:**
Forono, early blood turnip, eagle, ruby queen, Chicago red

# Corn

Around 1.2 billion tons (1.1 billion metric tons) of corn are harvested every year. This mind-boggling number corresponds to the weight of about 220 million adult elephants!

Sweetcorn is a special corn variety, and it's tasty and juicy in any form – raw, boiled or grilled. However, the favorite corn of many people is popcorn. Millions of pounds (or kg) of this famous snack are consumed every year!

Dried corn kernels become popcorn when they are put in a little oil, placed on high heat and then burst. People around the world can be heard crunching this puffed-up treat in movie theaters, parties or anywhere they're having fun. For some, however, eating popcorn in public can be a nuisance. The Knigge Society in Germany, which strives to encourage good manners, has tried for a long time to get a ban on popcorn, at least in theaters.

Popcorn is also good at absorbing the impact of crashes, so it's sometimes used as a filling material to protect items shipped in cardboard boxes. It is more environmentally-friendly than Styrofoam and plastic because, after doing its job with the mail, popcorn is easily degradable and can even be used as animal feed. Other types of corn can be used to make semolina and flour for dishes such as polenta and tortillas. Still others can help produce energy sources such as biogas and material for toys and handicrafts. You see, corn is truly multi-talented!

With its so many uses, we have to be careful that the whole world isn't soon covered in cornfields. Too much of any type of plant can bring nature out of balance, and corn is already the most commonly grown cereal – even ahead of wheat. By the way, if corn really is a cereal, then what is it doing in a book about vegetables? During the 16th century, European discoverers explored much of the world. They found continents they'd never seen before and caused a quite a lot of damage. But they also brought amazing things back home with them, such as corn. Over time, people in Europe and other places began to think of corn as a vegetable – even though the corn plant is related to crops such as wheat, barley or rye.

**Edible parts of the plant:**
Kernels from the cobs of sweetcorn can be eaten raw or cooked; while in other varieties, the kernels can be eaten as popcorn or ground into semolina.

**Tasty corn varieties:**
Trinity, honey select, silver choice, painted mountain, Buhl

# Sweet Potato

Although they both have nearly the same name, look equally stumpy and make for delicious French fries, potatoes and sweet potatoes are very different. The potato is a real nightshade plant that should only be eaten when cooked, while the sweet potato is fully non-toxic when raw. Even the leaves of this pretty, pink-flowered bindweed can be cooked just like spinach. In many countries, the plant's orange or purple-colored tubers are baked before eating. These tubers grow at the roots underground and can weigh up to two pounds (0.9 kg).

Recently, a 57-million-year-old fossil of a bindweed, an ancestor of the sweet potato, was discovered in India. What a sensation! Up until then, everyone thought that sweet potatoes originated in the Americas. But no matter where they first evolved, sweet potatoes have been cultivated by humans for a long time. People in the Rio Grande area of Peru, for example, were already growing them 5,800 years ago. George Washington, who was both a farmer and the first President of the United States, grew sweet potatoes at Muddy Hole farm, which was part of his huge Mount Vernon estate in Virginia.

Washington's namesake, George Washington Carver, was an African-American inventor who did much more with the sweet potato than offer it as a side dish at Thanksgiving. He came up with dozens of inventions for using the plant. Among these were glues for postage stamps, ink, shoe polish, a type of rayon, as well as ropes and dyes!

The sweet potato plant is not only versatile, it's also quite durable and can even survive artificial light. It is hardly surprising, therefore, that scientists from the NASA space agency have long packed them into their suitcases. When we finally make our way to Mars, the sweet potato will likely come with us!

**Edible parts of the plant:**
The tuber can be eaten raw and cooked, and the leaves are edible, too.

**Tasty varieties of sweet potato:**
Japanese, jewel, Ringley's Porto Rico

# Fennel

Fennel may just be the first vegetable you ever tried. And I don't mean the green-white, onion-like thing that grows in the garden. I'm referring to fennel tea, which is made from the dried plant. Your parents may have had you drink the tea from your baby bottle, because it helped you digest foot and kept you from farting too much! You may also have spat the fennel tea right back out. Some of us do not like the taste at all, while others love it… a disagreement that also applies to the similar-tasting licorice.

Babies and nursing mothers are not the only people who benefit from fennel. The plant has been used in many types of medicines since ancient times. The people of Mesopotamia used it as a medicinal plant over 5,000 years ago. Around 3,000 years later in ancient Greece, the famous doctor Hippocrates recommended its use against every imaginable complaint. By the way, the Greek word for fennel is 'marathon', a word you might recognize. The town of Marathon got its name from the surrounding fennel fields, and it became famous as the site where, according to legend, the first marathon run took place in 490 BC.

During the Middle Ages, fennel plants could be found in almost every monastery garden. The plant's onion-like bulb forms in thick layers from the leaves just above the ground, and it can be eaten raw or even cooked. The little fennel fruits and leaves, which can be easily dried and look like seeds, are picked for making tea and medications. They contain essential oils that can remedy stomach cramps and bad coughs. Fennel can even be used against snake bites.

In earlier times, people believed fennel had magic powers! On Midsummer's Day, shortly after the summer solstice at the end of June, fennel herbs were stuffed into keyholes. This was meant to ward off bad spirits throughout the whole year. I wouldn't try that trick with your front door, however. You might have a hard time fitting your key into the lock!

**Edible parts of the plant:**
All parts can be eaten, but we mainly prefer the onion-shaped tuber and the flowers.

**Tasty varieties:**
Grosfruchtiger, Zefa Fino, Florence, Romanesco

# Pumpkin, Cucumber and Zucchini

Weighing in at 2,623 pounds (1,190 kg), it's the heaviest berry in the world! No, it's not a joke. This heavyweight world record was set by a pumpkin in 2016. But is the pumpkin really a berry fruit? Plant experts already know the answer. Because a pumpkin grows out from the same yellow flower year after year, it is classified as a fruit. Moreover, because pumpkins have seeds and a fleshy pulp, they are categorized as berries as well. And what a tank of a berry the pumpkin is, with its thick, hard, armor-like shell. Smaller pumpkins, in fact, are often shot through the air like cannon balls. In the U.S. town of Millsboro, Delaware, this pumpkin 'war' takes place on the first weekend after Halloween. Inventors there have been competing against each other since 1986 to see how far they can shoot pumpkins with home-designed slingshots, catapults and air-pressure cannons. The best shot so far was 1,421 yards (1,300 meters).

You can, of course, do sensible things with pumpkins, such as carving scary lanterns that glow wonderfully orange in the dark. Or you can press the fruit's seeds into oil, roast them and then enjoy a pumpkin snack that's healthier than potato chips. Pumpkin risotto, an Italian dish with pumpkin and rice, is also delicious. Italians call a regular-sized pumpkin 'zucca', while a smaller version is referred to as 'zucchino' (pronounced like *zukino*). And this brings us to the smaller siblings of the pumpkin, namely the zucchini. These berries can also get really big, but the smaller, more delicate ones taste much better. Besides, unhealthy, bitter substances develop in zucchini the longer you let them grow. Zucchini flowers are also edible, and they can be stuffed and fried to make a real delicacy.

Though normally long and green, zucchini are also available in yellow and in a circular shape. When you visit a supermarket, you'll probably discover that green zucchini and cucumbers look quite similar. That's because the two berries are closely related. Cucumbers contain up to 97% water and are a popular food. But they can also serve other purposes, such as cleaning shoes, mirrors and sinks, and removing mouth odor and ink stains.

**Edible parts of the plants:**
For all three, people eat the flesh. Pumpkins are cooked, cucumbers are eaten raw and zucchini is consumed both ways. Zucchini flowers are also prized as a delicacy.

**Some varieties of these berries:**
Rouge vif d'Etampes, ghost rider, Kakai pumpkins; Sikkim, Viridis, muncher, Japanese long cucumbers; raven, Ronde de Nice, Italiano largo zucchini

# Broccoli

There are some very unusual holidays! Have you heard of World Bubble Day on October 5th or National Tooth Fairy Day on February 28th? Two days are even dedicated to broccoli, one of the superheroes among vegetables: St. Broccoli Day on March 18th and the National We Love Broccoli Day on March 22nd (which is the same day as National Goof-Off Day!).

Broccoli lovers prepare healthy dishes from the stems and florets of this green flower. There is twice as much vitamin C in broccoli as there is in an orange, along with a heap of other vitamins, minerals, iron, and fiber – and all this comes with virtually no calories. Broccoli gives people strength and perks them up when they are tired. It may even help treat disease. Heidelberg University Hospital in Germany is currently researching to what extent broccoli's natural ingredients can be used in cancer therapies. Broccoli is truly a vegetable hero, which is why people like it on their plate!

The world record holder in broccoli speed eating, Tom Lander, can devour two-thirds of a pound (one-third of a kg) in an incredible 92 seconds. For people in Germany who want to train for this contest, there's an easy way to determine the weight of the broccoli they're eating. That's because almost every head of broccoli in German supermarkets weighs about 12 ounces (340 grams). In other countries, buyers must decide between heads of different sizes and weights. All of this means that broccoli harvesters in Germany must have a good sense of proportion when deciding which stems they are about to cut off and which ones may need a little more growing time. But they must avoid letting them grow too long, as the florets of the broccoli heads will open up and produce bright yellow blossoms.

The word broccoli comes from an Italian term meaning 'the flowering crest of the cabbage'. Incidentally, there would be no James Bond films without broccoli. This, of course, doesn't mean that the actors who played Agent 007 stayed fit because they always ate their broccoli. The producer of the first Bond films was named Albert Broccoli.

**Edible parts of the plant:**
The head and stem can be eaten raw or cooked, sometimes with the fine leaves and shoots that come from the seeds.

**Varieties of broccoli:**
dia green, quarantina, Calabria, Arcadia

# Asparagus

If you live in Germany, Austria or other parts of Europe, you're sure to have seen white asparagus spears with their little buds go on sale each spring. Grown-ups there go crazy for them and are constantly preparing meals until the end of 'white asparagus season'. This vegetable is often boiled or pan-fried, as its intense flavor tastes best when cooked, though some asparagus can be eaten raw in a salad. Kids, on the other hand, often tend to be less fond of this sometimes bitter vegetable.

Nevertheless, it's worth giving asparagus a go and then trying something out later – when you're in the bathroom. There's an important thing to know about asparagus: the shoots of the plant contain a diuretic called aspartic acid. Anyone who eats asparagus brings their kidneys to 'life' and soon needs to use the bathroom to pee. And when you pee, the smell can be pretty disgusting because the body converts aspartic acid into sulfur compounds. Smelly asparagus pee has an odor similar to skunk liquid, though not quite so strong. Some people, however, do not smell a thing in the bathroom after eating asparagus. There can be two very different reasons for this: either they are missing a certain receptor in the nose, or their kidneys process the substances in asparagus without producing sulfur compounds. Only 40% of people genetically become asparagus skunks.

Farmers typically stop cutting and gathering asparagus in the summer, and they then allow the roots the peace they need to grow nicely again for the following year. Asparagus, in fact, belongs to a group of vegetables we call perennials. They can continue sprouting from their roots for up to ten years. Rows of soil are piled on top of the white asparagus to ensure they are not exposed to any sunlight. The buds of green asparagus, however, are allowed to stick out above the ground and create chlorophyll (a natural green pigment) before they are cut with a special knife. Because this harvesting can only be done by hand, and because the plants need a lot of space to grow, asparagus is one of the most expensive vegetables in the store.

In earlier times, people ate asparagus with their hands – even those in the most elegant societies. This custom arose because chemicals in asparagus turned silver forks and knives black. It's a shame that most cutlery nowadays is made of stainless steel, and that we no longer have such a good excuse for eating asparagus in a fun way!

**Edible parts of the plant:**
The fleshy spears from the root taste more flavorful when cooked, but they can also be eaten raw.

**Tasty varieties:**
Larac, Asperges d'Argenteuil, Jersey knight, Guelph millennium

# Peas and Beans

Do you know the funny children's song that goes 'Beans, beans, the musical fruit; the more you eat, the more you toot…'? As healthy as beans are, they contain hard-to-digest carbohydrates. Beans get broken down by bacteria in the body, which produces gases within the intestine. These gases have to leave the body to prevent sickness … and when they leave, they often make quite a musical 'toot', or fart!

There are thousands of bean varieties all over the world. Depending on the variety, you can eat either the seeds from the bean plant or the entire seed pods with the seeds in them. One thing, however, is essential. Never, never, ever eat beans before they have been cooked! In their uncooked state, they contain a poison called lectin, which can be especially harmful for kids, even in small amounts. This poison is completely destroyed when the beans are cooked.  What remains are valuable ingredients, some of which can also replace meat. Not surprisingly, beans rank among the most important vegetables and have been cultivated for more than 10,000 years. They also have popular plant sisters – the peas! People worldwide enjoy the seeds of round and wrinkled peas, or even the entire bright green shells of unripe harvested sugar peas. In contrast to kidney-shaped beans, the spherical pea seeds are not unhealthy when eaten raw.

You should never confuse real peas with chick peas. Both are in the legume family of plants, and both are popular foods. But each belongs to a different part of that family (or, as scientists would say, a different 'genus'). The word chick comes from the Latin 'cicer', which means both 'pea' and 'to giggle'. And as with beans and other shell fruit, there's definitely a fart alert after eating chick peas. There is some good news, however, when it comes to this problem. British biologist Colin Leakey has cultivated a bean variety that does not cause gas!

**Edible parts of the plants:**
The seeds and the unripe, harvested bean shells are eaten – but they must be cooked!
Real peas (not chick peas) can be consumed raw.

**Varieties of these seed vegetables:**
empress, mrociumere (originally from Kenya), tobacco worm, willow leaf lima beans
Cascadia, Piccolo Provenzale, Mayfair, white acre, sugar snap peas

# Onion, Garlic and Leek

In some countries, people insult others by calling them a 'leek'. Maybe this put-down has something to do with the leek vegetable's appearance, with its narrow-chested shape and funny, ragged-looking hairstyle. Leeks, however, have every reason to be proud of themselves! For thousands of years, they have been highly prized for their versatile qualities, as a staple foodstuff, and even more so for medicinal reasons.

In ancient Egypt, the workers building the pyramids were paid in onions and garlic, among other things. Greek athletes strengthened themselves for the Olympic Games using these vegetables. Later on, leeks arrived in northern Europe in the backpacks of Roman soldiers. Ancient healers and doctors once used them for inflammation, fever, skin rashes, heart problems, mosquito bites, snake bites and other sicknesses! Hair loss, too, was treated with garlic! Today, people still place their trust in the healing effects of sulfur compounds found in members of the leek family, and you can buy shampoo with garlic extract in it. These healthy vegetables can also serve other purposes. If you drop a bowl in the bathroom, you can clean the tiles with half an onion and glue the pieces together with the juice of a garlic clove. It's no joke, it works!

Many of us like the taste of leek, onion and garlic in spite of the lingering bad breath that usually occurs after eating them. We also may have to shed tears when chopping onions, though the sharpest possible knife will help counteract this effect. Sharp knives reduce the number of onion cells that are crushed when onion cutting, and it's these crushed cells that release vapors to irritate our eyes. Or, if you don't have sharp-enough cutlery, you could always try wearing diving goggles!

**Edible parts of the plants:**
The thickened bulb of the shoot above the onion root can be eaten raw, while the garlic clove is enjoyed raw, fried or boiled. With leeks, the entire shaft can be consumed, including the green leaves, though the darker green part at the end of the shaft is too hard to be eaten raw. But be sure to heed this warning – leeks are poisonous for dogs and cats whether raw or cooked!

**Varieties:**
Barletta, Cipollotto da Mazzi, red wing, Stuttgarter onions
Bogatyr, Persian star, Blanco Piacenza, Killarney red, Shantung purple garlic
Musselburgh, Gigante d'Inverno, Lincoln, Lancelot, imperial leeks

# Tomato

Though classified as a fruit by scientists, the tomato is enjoyed as a vegetable by cooks and eaters alike — by far the most popular vegetable in the world. Tomatoes were actually considered poisonous in most countries up to the beginning of the last century! People in Latin America, however, had known better for a long time. They'd grown tomatoes for thousands of years in Mexico and Peru, using the plants for food and medicines. The Aztecs of Mexico called them 'Xitomatl', a name in which the modern word 'tomato' can be clearly recognized.

Around 1500, Spanish seafarers brought tomatoes back to Europe for the first time. The tomato berries of that period were yellow and cherry-sized; and although they were attractive to the eye, they were also highly untrustworthy. After all, tomatoes originate from the nightshade family and have many poisonous relatives. The tomato plant, however, only contains the toxin solanine in its green parts, and only to a small degree. Nevertheless, there were a number of deadly accidents with tomatoes. Noblemen had eaten them and died. Today, historians believe the tomato's acids, harmless in themselves, helped secrete life-threatening lead compounds from the pewter plates that once graced wealthy dinner tables. People at that time did not know about lead poisoning, so they labeled the tomato a poisonous plant and preferred to grow it only in ornamental gardens.

Not all Europeans, however, were afraid of tomatoes. In Italy, cooks experimented with the 'pomodori' — the golden apple. It often pops up as a rare ingredient in very old cookbooks. But the tomato only made its real breakthrough just over 200 years ago on the pizza. Since then, it has only become more and more popular. Well over 3,000 varieties are being grown today in all different colors, shapes and types. They can be white, yellow, green, red or even black in hue, some with freckles and some with zebra stripes, and they can have round, oval or fluted shapes. There are cocktail tomatoes as small as cherries and beefsteak tomatoes that can weigh up to two pounds (0.9 kg) or more.

At the Spanish city of Buñol, the crazy Tomatina festival takes place in August. More than 20,000 people have overripe tomatoes thrown at them for an hour! Other people use tomatoes in more sensible ways. Plastics made from tomato seeds, skins and stems may soon be used to build cars.

**Edible parts of the plant:**
The fruit, or in this case, the berry, can be enjoyed in any state.

**Tasty varieties of tomato:**
cherry Roma, Polish, Granadero, red cherry, black pearl, Fiaschetto di Manduria

# Bell Pepper, Capsicum and Chili

Christopher Columbus embarked on his famous sea voyage in 1492. He was trying to reach India in search of pepper and other spices. When he and his crew found land, they went ashore and discovered a spice that did not specifically look like a pepper, but tasted at least as hot. Columbus had not only sailed to America by accident, he had also found a pepper unknown to Europeans. He named this tart fruit 'pimiento', which is the Spanish word for pepper. Today, pepper types from all over the world have a variation of the word pepper in their name, whether it is 'biber' in Turkish, 'paprika' in Hungarian or 'poivron' in French.

After Columbus's voyages, Spanish seafarers brought many edible plants back with them from South America during their not always peaceful discovery tours of the 16th century. Bell pepper, capsicum and chili are all different types of the pepper plant. We eat these fruits raw, cooked, dried and ground as a spice. However, please pay attention because the berries of the pepper can be uncomfortable on the tongue! And like all nightshade plants, the green parts of the plant contain the toxin solanine. That is why the ripe red peppers are easier to digest than the still unripe green and the half-ripe yellow ones.

When it comes to protecting peppers from unwanted enemies, nature has come up with a very special protection plan called capsaicin. This chemical puts plenty of fire in your mouth, especially with chilies. Birds do not detect it, but insects and mammals are driven away by its sharpness. Chili extract prevents rodents from gnawing away at the casings of fiber optic cables, and mussels refrain from attaching themselves to the hulls of ships that have been painted with chili paint. Only humans seem drawn to the fiery zing of chilies. When we eat them, our body responds to the pain by releasing 'happiness' hormones in our brains. Chilies, in fact, are being cultivated to be hotter than ever! Humans also use capsicum for more aggressive purposes – including pepper spray.

**Edible plant parts:**
The pepper is also a berry fruit, and the entire berry is enjoyable raw or cooked and dried as a spice.

**Tasty (and hot!) varieties of peppers:**
Cayenne long (very hot), jalapeño (hot), Margaret's (sweet), chili grande (hot), Rocoto (hot capsicum), golden bell (sweet)

# Spinach and Chard

Spinach does not seem all that exciting at first glance, with its ordinary green leaves, light-green flowers and small fruits. Even its name, which comes from 'spina', a Latin word for 'thorn', suggests the plant's lowly, humble appearance. By contrast, spinach's bigger brother chard stands erect and proud in forests and gardens. Its strong and wavy leaves sit upon white, yellow, orange and red stems. Chard is not only beautiful to behold, it's also versatile and delicious.

But why has there been so much more interest in spinach over the last 100 years? Well, it's because this humble-looking vegetable has all kinds of amazing powers. Scientists can add microscopic particles to spinach and use it to detect explosives in groundwater. Other researchers are trying to create artificial heart tissue from the plant. And we can't forget Popeye, the famous comic book hero who got his superpowers merely by gulping down one can of cooked spinach! American cartoonist E.C. Segar created Popeye in the 1920's, a time when parents tried to feed their babies more and more of the green vegetable. They were told that spinach was important nutrition for infants because it contained a large amount of iron. Later on, it became clear that only dried spinach possessed unusually high levels of iron. Raw spinach, as well as chard, has about as much iron as in lentils and beans, and significantly less than in mushrooms. Moreover, the amount of iron in cooked spinach is 90% less than people believed in Segar's day, when cooked spinach was the most popular form of the vegetable.

And yet, there is something true about the fairy tale of the spinach-fueled Popeye. According to the latest research, spinach contains another ingredient that is good for muscle building. There is even a debate as to whether this substance should be placed on the list of prohibited doping agents for athletes. Fortunately, Olympic runners and swimmers can still enjoy spinach. That's because you would have to eat 14 pounds (6.3 kg) of spinach a day to be illegally doped. And with such a full stomach, you wouldn't be able to climb onto the winner's podium anyway!

**Edible parts of the plants:**
The leaves and stems are eaten raw and cooked, as are the seeds.

**Varieties of spinach and chard:**
Giant winter, baby's leaf, Bordeaux spinach
Burpee's rhubarb, Verte a Carde Blanche, Verde da Taglio chards

# Potato

It was venerated as sacred in South America for more than 13 millennia, yet damned as the devil's food in Europe only three hundred years ago. Yes, we're talking about a very famous tuber – the potato! One reason Europeans vilified potatoes was because they tried to eat the plant's toxic leaves and flowers, rather than the modest tuber underground. When they realized their mistake, people throughout Europe soon became potato lovers. The tuber became so important that Prussia's King Frederick the Great ordered it to be grown on a large scale in 1748 to prevent famine.

Whether in the form of dumplings, mash, pancakes, gratins, fries or simply the boiled tuber, potatoes are now valued worldwide. In recent years, however, the potato boom has faded a bit in some countries. People are more health conscious these days, and there are worries that potatoes may make you fat. Anyone saying that, though, is not doing the potato any justice. The only problem lies in the way the tubers are prepared. Of course, French fries dripping with oil are not healthy for anyone. But when we look at a baked potato, 3.5 ounces (99 grams) of the food have only a fifth as many calories as the same amount of pasta. Even rice is not as calorie-light as that. And unlike pasta, potatoes have a lot of vitamin C and other valuable nutrients.

What's more, potatoes have other superpowers unrelated to food. There's an amazing variety of things you can make from potatoes and the starch they contain: paper, wallpaper paste, Scotch tape, shampoo, soap, laundry powder and batteries. Even artificial snow made from potatoes has been used for about 15 years in the production of movies. It's no wonder that vast amounts of potatoes are being grown around the world today.

As we've said before, the most useful part of the potato is the gnarled tuber growing underground, which is often brown but can also be red or purple in color. There are more than 5,000 varieties of this adaptable nightshade plant.

**Edible parts of the plant:**
The tuber can be eaten cooked – never raw!

**Varieties of potato:**
Satina, daisy gold, purple Viking, French fingerling, dark red Norland, russet Norkotah

# Radicchio

The name radicchio comes from Italian and, roughly translated, means 'little root'. The best-known type is probably the radicchio di Chioggia, whose red-white leaves make salads look prettier. But there are plenty of other types, shapes and colors. There are green ones with red-green speckles and white ones with deep purple spots. However, don't be deceived by its cheerful coloring. The radicchio can be quite a bitter little fellow. Most children do not like its taste, which isn't a bad thing because bitter substances are often a sign that a plant is not agreeable or safe to eat. But the radicchio contains ingredients that make people healthier and aid in food digestion. The older people get, the more they like the radicchio's bitter taste – and it's the older folks whose bodies need its healthy substances the most.

But if you don't like the radicchio's bitterness, it can be taken out of the leaves by soaking them in water for half an hour before consuming them. You can also focus on the red parts of the root, which are milder than the white stems. When cooked, radicchio can have an almost sweet taste. I know someone who makes radicchio marmalade that goes especially well with cheese.

But why is this vegetable called 'little root', when we only eat the leaf part of the plant? In Italy, where radicchio got its name and where much of it is grown, people keenly consume the plant's carrot-shaped roots. They are bitterer than the part above ground, and their popularity does not extend beyond Italy's borders.

Radicchio has a number of plant relatives, including chicory, which has noticeably thicker roots. Chicory is harvested in the fall, and the cut leaves are left in the dark to form new buds. These whitish buds taste somewhat milder than radicchio. Chicory roots were traditionally thrown away after harvest, but there has recently been a fantastic discovery. Extracts from the roots can be used in the production of plastics such as nylon and polyester. Maybe some of your clothes contain a bit of the radicchio family in them!

**Edible parts of the plant:**
The leaves and even the entire head and stalk are eaten raw or cooked,
but people rarely consume the roots.

**Varieties:**
Radicchio di Chioggia, Treviso, Rossa di Verona

# Veggie Art

## or what Olaf Hajek thinks about taste and vegetables.

Painting vegetables is an adventure! Our artist, Olaf Hajek, instantly thinks of the colorful, miraculous shapes we see in sunny, yellow cobs of corn and fluffy fennel. At first glance, he is not especially taken with some types of vegetables, such as the brown potato tuber or the chubby eggplant. Nonetheless, all of them are given access to his shopping basket when he visits the market in Palma de Majorca, Spain. For when it comes to eating, Olaf loves all vegetables. He prefers, however, to buy those types that are unfamiliar to him – oddly speckled green tomatoes, for example. How many surprises are missed when people automatically decide to dislike something? Olaf feels sorry for those who are not inquisitive. Their life is so limited in contrast with people who take a risk now and then!

Once home, Olaf unpacks his treasures and looks through his many cookbooks. He then puts them to one side and cooks whatever springs to mind. Strictly following recipes is not his thing. Olaf doesn't want to know in advance exactly what's going to end up on his table. That would be a little bit boring, wouldn't it? When experimenting with vegetables and spices, Olaf knows one thing for certain, namely that his plate will be bursting with something special, something with enough energy to surprise him, and something that gives him the power to do somersaults.

And how does Olaf paint his veggie pictures? Before he handles radicchio, for example, he observes it very carefully and then listens to his heart. It's best for him not to know too much about the origin and characteristics of this salad plant. The ideas for his paintings must arise from deep within his imagination. So what does he think of when first looking at the radicchio's red-veined, stretched-out leaves? Sumptuous fabrics... patterns... exactly – a dress! An evening gown for a famous diva! And then, instead of going for his salad strainer, Olaf quickly picks up his brush and acrylic paint, sketches the outline of the vegetable at the center of his picture, and begins to paint. You'd think a couple of salad leaves would be insufficient to create a whole skirt. But that's exactly why Olaf tries to do it!

Olaf's pictures always require a second look. Does his vegetable look normal, or is the person too small? Or does the person look normal and the vegetable much too big? Everything is possible with art and nothing is out of place. In Olaf's imagination, circus acrobats and animals dance around enormous tubers, berries and turnips. And that's because vegetables are the very things that make people and animals so strong and skillful. A well-to-do fellow would have his potatoes served to him like treasures, while a clumsy drake would carry the weight of a corn cob on its back just to lure the tender chicks behind him.

An illustrator, which is the best word to define Olaf's profession, usually paints explanatory pictures to accompany a text. This word, however, is derived from an ancient Latin term, 'illustrare', which means 'to illuminate, brighten and praise' – a far more fitting description of Olaf's pictures. He celebrates vegetables in this book as if they were superheroes. And, indeed, he is a 'super' illustrator, who since childhood never wanted to do anything other than what he does now.

Do you like painting, too? Maybe you feel uncertain that what you've painted has not turned out so well? If so, here is a solid piece of advice from Olaf. It's better to paint what you imagine than what you see before you – even if the horse's back is too long or the pooch's front paws are too big. It is not so important that animals, people, objects and vegetables look real in works of art. You might as well take a photo of them instead! If you think you're unable to paint something, just let it be. The main thing is that you find harmony in your picture when you're done. In other words, the work should have a kind of perfection in your own eyes. And should someone complain that they do not like your artwork, simply answer: 'There's no squabbling about taste – not even about the taste of red beets. Best Wishes from Olaf Hajek!'

# The Vegetables in this Book

© 2021, Prestel Verlag, Munich · London · New York
A member of Penguin Random House Verlagsgruppe GmbH
Neumarkter Strasse 28 · 81673 Munich

© for the illustrations: Olaf Hajek
© for the text: Annette Roeder

Library of Congress Control Number: 2020948529
A CIP catalogue record for this book is available from the British Library.
Library of Congress Cataloging-in-Publication Data

Translated from the German by Paul Kelly

Editorial direction: Doris Kutschbach
Copyediting: Brad Finger
Production management: Susanne Hermann
Layout and typesetting: Meike Sellier
Separations: Reproline mediateam, Munich
Printing and binding: DZS Grafik d.o.o.

Prestel Publishing compensates the $CO_2$ emissions produced from the making
of this book by supporting a reforestation project in Brazil. Find further information
on the project here: www.ClimatePartner.com/14044-1912-1001

Penguin Random House
Verlagsgruppe FSC® N001967

Printed in Slovenia

ISBN 978-3-7913-7478–9
www.prestel.com